WARMED BY BEES

Sue Hamilton

VISIT US AT

WWW.ABDOPUBLISHING.COM

Published by ABDO Publishing Company, 8000 West 78th Street, Suite 310, Edina, MN 55439. Copyright ©2010 by Abdo Consulting Group, Inc. International copyrights reserved in all countries. No part of this book may be reproduced in any form without written permission from the publisher. ABDO & Daughters™ is a trademark and logo of ABDO Publishing Company.

Printed in the United States of America, North Mankato, Minnesota.
112009
012010

♻ PRINTED ON RECYCLED PAPER

Editor & Cover Design: John Hamilton
Graphic Design: Sue Hamilton
Cover Photo: iStockphoto
Interior Photos and Illustrations: ALK EpiPen, p. 28; AP Images, p. 11, 12, 17; Gary Friedman, p. 16; Getty Images, p. 1, 19, 20, 21, 27; iStockphoto, p. 13, 14; Jupiterimages, p. 6; Photo Researchers, p. 3, 4, 5, 7, 8, 9, 10, 22, 23, 24, 25, 26, 29; Visuals Unlimited, p. 8, 15, 18, 32.

Library of Congress Cataloging-in-Publication Data

Hamilton, Sue L., 1959-
  Swarmed by bees / Sue Hamilton.
    p. cm. -- (Close encounters of the wild kind)
  Includes index.
  ISBN 978-1-60453-933-2
  1. Bee attacks--Juvenile literature. 2. Bees--Swarming--Juvenile literature. I. Title.
  QL565.2.H355 2010
  595.79'915--dc22
                    2009045598

CONTENTS

DEATH STINGS

Bees—there are billions of them, and they are found on every continent except Antarctica. They not only create honey, they also play a vital role in pollinating the crops and trees that keep the world fed.

Bees work together to create a successful hive, and they are willing to die to protect it. Unlucky people who disturb hives may find themselves covered by thousands of buzzing, mad insects within seconds. And each bee is armed with a stinger capable of injecting a powerful toxin.

For some people, time spent outdoors can quickly turn life threatening. Human reaction to bee venom ranges from minor pain and swelling to frightening anaphylactic shock, in which the victim stops breathing. In the United States, bee stings cause more deaths per year than any other creature.

Right: A woman shows her normal hand size and the swollen effect of a bee sting on the other hand. *Facing page:* Honeybees work cooperatively in their hive.

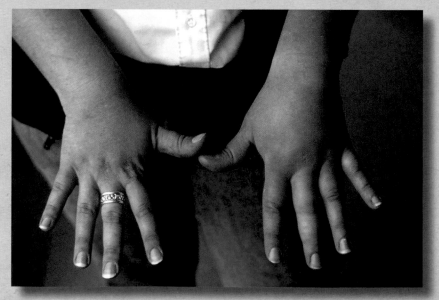

BEE SENSES

Bees can easily see movement, like flowers blowing in the wind, or intruders near their hive. But their eyesight is only fair, and they have poor depth perception. They sometimes collide with each other when flying in and out of their hive. Bee experts compare looking through the eyes of a honeybee to looking through a wall of glass bricks.

Luckily for bees, their survival depends more on their keen sense of smell than their poor eyesight. Bees use sharp olfactory (smell) receptors found in their antennae to distinguish odors. They use their sense of smell to communicate their location to other bees, and to find food, choosing their favorite flowers and plants.

When threatened or squashed by a panicked human, bees give off a special chemical substance called an alarm pheromone. The smell is vaguely banana-like to humans, but to bees it means that the hive is in trouble and needs help. Hundreds, even thousands, of bees will immediately respond to the smell, attacking whatever has threatened their home, human or animal, with fierce, unrelenting vengeance.

Above: Bees see movement like flowers blowing in the wind, but mostly they use the smell receptors in their antennae to find their favorite flowers and plants.

A close-up image of a bee head.

STINGERS AND VENOM

When defending their hive against people and other thick-skinned mammals, honeybees are on a suicide mission. They attack, sting, and die. The barbed stinger sticks into the thick-skinned victim, ripping out of the bee. The bee flies away to die. The stinger and venom gland remain, continuing to shoot poison into the victim's bloodstream for another 10 to 20 seconds.

Wasps, on the other hand, have sharp, smooth stingers that easily move in and out of human flesh. Curving its abdomen, a wasp uses strong muscles to shove the hypodermic-like stinger deep into its victim's skin. Poison shoots from a venom sac inside the insect into a victim's bloodstream. A wasp can sting an unlucky person again and again.

 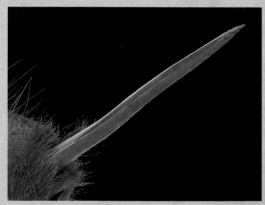

A close-up of a bee's barbed stinger. When a bee stings a human, the barb sticks in the flesh. When the bee flies away, the stinger and venom gland rip out and the bee dies.

A close-up of a wasp's smooth stinger. The wasp's sharp, smooth stinger allows the insect to sting a person again and again.

A bee's stinger and venom gland remain after the bee has stung a person.

> "All the honey a bee gathers during its lifetime doesn't sweeten its sting."
> —Italian Proverb

For most victims, a sting causes pain and swelling at the injection site. They may require no medical treatment other than an over-the-counter antihistamine, such as Benadryl. However, for people who are highly allergic, or are stung multiple times, bee venom can be fatal.

Bee venom can cause an extreme reaction called anaphylaxis. Victims experience a rapid drop in blood pressure. They have trouble breathing and swallowing. The tissue around their lips and eyes becomes swollen. They may vomit or faint. Anaphylaxis is frightening and quick. Most deaths happen within an hour of being stung.

About 100 deaths occur each year in the United States from reactions to bee stings. Some people die from a single sting. Others survive even after being swarmed and stung more than 1,000 times. What victims do to help themselves during and after a bee attack can mean the difference between life and death.

Right: A woman's eye begins to swell shut after a bee sting. The swelling and redness are the body's reaction to the bee's venom. This kind of hyper-sensitive reaction is called an anaphylactic response. The pain, redness, and swelling may last for up to 48 hours.

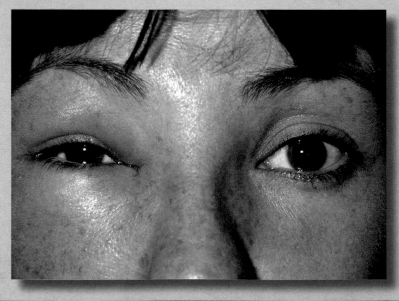

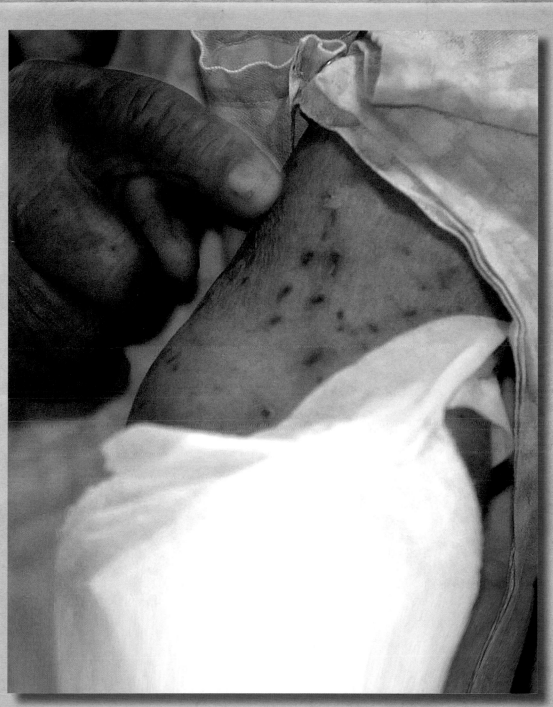

Above: A man shows some of the marks made by the more than 1,000 Africanized bees that attacked him while working on his ranch in Texas. It took four people two hours to remove the stingers left by the aggressive bees. It's estimated that people can survive up to 10 bee stings per pound of body weight. But for people who are allergic to bee venom, one sting can be deadly.

AFRICANIZED BEES

Africanized bees are a cross between African and European honeybees. They were brought together as part of an experiment conducted by scientists in South America in the late 1950s. Entomologists were trying to breed a better honeybee. The result was a stronger but much more aggressive bee. These hybrid bees were accidentally released into the area. Over the years, swarms of these "killer bees" have thrived, even migrating as far as the southern United States.

On September 16, 2009, Justin Otton was clearing weeds with a tractor near a canal in San Elizario, a town near El Paso, Texas. Otton didn't know an Africanized bee hive was in the area. The windows of his tractor were open. Suddenly, the 35-year-old worker was attacked by angry bees.

Right: Africanized bees, also known as killer bees, are a much stronger and more aggressive bee.
Facing page: Thousands of bees swarm together on a tree. A hive of honeybees may consist of up to 20,000 bees. If threatened, they will all attack at once.

> "Hospital staff estimated Justin Otton had been stung approximately 200 to 300 times in the head, neck, face, and hands."
>
> —El Paso Sheriff's Office, September 16, 2009, San Elizario, TX

Known for their aggressive nature, Africanized honeybees attack with speed and power. Inside the open cab of the tractor, Otton was quickly covered with the buzzing, stinging insects. He had no choice but to run.

Bees do not give up until a threat is gone from the area. Otton was chased into the street, where a car with two men inside stopped and tried to help the unlucky worker. The bees stung them, too. With bees swarming, they couldn't even get back in their car. They had to run, too.

Luckily, none of the three men died from the bee stings. With hundreds of stings on his head and body, Otton was treated at a local hospital. Ambulance workers helped the other two men. Since the hive was in a public area, firefighters later destroyed the nest.

The aggressive nature of Africanized bees makes it vital for anyone to get away from the creatures as quickly as possible. Do not swat at them. That only releases their alarm pheromone and further infuriates the insects. Cover your eyes, nose, and throat as much as possible, and run!

Right: When bees attack, the only defense is to get away. Run away as fast as possible. Do not swat at the bees. *Facing page:* Killer bees are known for their aggressive nature. They will protect their nest and they will attack anyone who disturbs them.

BUMBLEBEE ATTACK

Bumblebees are fuzzy, black-and-yellow bees that prefer to avoid humans. When approached, they often fly away. However, if their nest is attacked, they will defend themselves. And their non-barbed stingers allow bumblebees to sting a victim again and again. In 1987, the California Highway Patrol discovered the aggressiveness of mad bumblebees while trying to help an accident victim near the San Diego Freeway.

On September 8, 1987, two people were involved in an early-morning car accident. The driver hit the shoulder of the freeway and plunged down an embankment. The car rolled to its side, sliding to a stop when the roof of the vehicle slammed into a eucalyptus tree. The driver was killed. The passenger, Josephina Pinosa, survived, but was knocked unconscious. The problem was, the tree was home to a hive of bumblebees. And they were fighting mad that their nest had been disturbed.

Right: The California Highway Patrol had to deal with both an accident victim and some very angry bumblebees after a car crash off the San Diego Freeway in 1987.

Above: A bumblebee on a coneflower. Bumblebees prefer to avoid humans, but if their nest is disturbed, they will attack. Bumblebees can sting a victim repeatedly.

When police, firefighters, and rescue crews arrived at the scene, they knew there was a live victim trapped in a crushed car down a hill. The location and damage to the car already made the rescue difficult—they would have to cut the woman from the crumpled car, which was partially wrapped around a tree.

Quickly, paramedics went down the embankment to give Pinosa oxygen and fluids while rescue crews powered up their tools to cut the woman out of the car. Suddenly, the air was filled with buzzing as the bumblebees took flight and began stinging. To make matters worse, the sound of the power tools infuriated another nearby nest. "You'd see them off a distance gathering, and then they'd come in again," said Battalion Chief Allen White of the Westminster Fire Department. "We had guys getting stung for an hour and a half."

Above: The head of a bumblebee.

> "They were just attacking like jets coming off an aircraft carrier."
> —Chief White, Westminster Fire Department, September 7, 1987, San Diego Freeway, California

Above: A bumblebee in flight.

The woman was badly hurt, and the firefighters had to keep working. Some were stung multiple times. White said, "The guys just kept working. It was miserable." The rescuers kept going until Pinosa was freed from the vehicle. Surviving both the accident and the bees, the 40-year-old woman was immediately transported to a nearby hospital for treatment.

On this day, emergency workers discovered the incredible pain and difficulty of working when a cloud of angry bumblebees is in the area. A couple of rescuers, however, weren't stung at all. By not swatting at the bees, they escaped the insects' wrath. As for the bees, after the car was towed off they went back to their daily business of collecting food and pollinating plants.

Above: A bumblebee flies out of its nest in the ground.

Above: A bumblebee's stinger.

WASP ATTACK

Wasps are sometimes called yellow jackets or hornets. They feed on other insects, including spiders and bees. Only females have stingers, which they usually use to paralyze their prey. Both males and females have biting mouthparts. Some wasps live alone, while others live in nests. These nests may be found in the ground, high in tree branches, or on homes.

Wasps are important. They control insect populations in the areas where they live. However, they can become aggressive towards people. This usually happens in late summer, after they are no longer rearing their young and are feeding on over-ripe, fermented fruits. When they attack, their stings are painful, and they can sting repeatedly. In 2009, Sarah Rayner learned this the hard way while rescuing 10-year-old Callum Grout from a wasp attack.

Right: A wasp nest in bushes. Wasps will attack when their nest is threatened or disturbed.
Facing page: A European wasp. Because of their smooth stinger, wasps are able to sting a person repeatedly.

On August 17, 2009, Rayner was sitting outdoors at a local pub in Peterborough, England, when she heard a child screaming for help. She rushed over to a nearby field, where she discovered a boy nearly covered in a black swarm of angry, stinging wasps.

Callum had gone to retrieve his football after it fell in a bush. He did not realize that the ball had landed on a wasps' nest. When the boy bent to grab the ball from the bush, the angry insects attacked. Quickly overcome by the painful stings, Callum fell to the ground, screaming as the wasps covered him.

Although fearful of wasps, Rayner didn't pause. She grabbed the wasp-covered boy, but also accidentally stepped on the nest. The rescuer quickly became a victim, receiving 20 stings to her foot, as well as additional stings to her body. She finally managed to drag herself and the boy away from the area.

Both victims survived the attack, although Rayner had an allergic reaction to the wasps' venom and had trouble breathing, which required a trip to the local hospital for treatment. Rayner stated, "It was very painful. Most of the stings were on my feet, but I also had a fair few under my arms as I pulled Callum from the bush."

The 10-year-old survived the attack, calling Rayner a hero. The boy now knows to look and listen for wasps when he's playing outside. And if wasps are around, Callum plans to run away as quickly as he can.

Right: The swollen hand of a woman who was stung by a wasp. The sting is near her wrist.

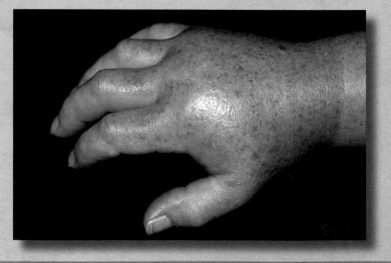

"When I got to Callum, he was covered from head to toe, and I knew I had to do something."

—Sarah Rayner, Rescuer and Victim of Wasp Attack, August 17, 2009, Peterborough, Cambridgeshire, England

Wasps in flight.

SURVIVING A SWARM

Bees are an important part of our world. It is estimated that their pollination results in 15 to 30 percent of the food eaten by people in the United States. While they only sting to defend themselves or to protect their nests, their venom can kill humans. Understanding what to do in case of a bee attack can save both bees and people.

First, be aware of your surroundings. Watch for bees coming in and out of an opening in a tree or the ground. Listen for the hum of activity from a hive. Do not stay in an area where there is heavy bee activity. It only takes one bee releasing its alarm pheromone to mark a victim and alert the entire hive.

Right: A wild honeybee hive in a forest. When hiking in the woods, be aware of your surroundings. Do not disturb a bees' nest, but if you do, be prepared to run away.

Next, if you find yourself suddenly attacked—RUN! Bees tend to go for the head and face. They are attracted to the carbon dioxide mammals breathe out. They will fly into your eyes, nose, and mouth and sting you there. It is not only difficult to run with bees covering your face, but stings inside the mouth and throat may cause swelling and quickly begin to make breathing difficult. Cover your head with your shirt or a jacket and run. Stings to the face are more dangerous than stings to the body.

Keep running. Bees have been known to chase people as far as one mile (1.6 km), but most quit after a quarter mile (.4 km). Keep going until you are safely away, or inside an enclosed building, tent, or car. Bees fly at speeds of 12 to 15 miles per hour (19 to 24 kph). Most people can outrun them.

Do not hide in water. Bees will wait patiently, then sting you every time you come up for air.

Do not swat at the bees. Every time you do, their alarm pheromone is released, further angering the bees.

Above: If bees attack, do not lay down. Get up and RUN!

27

IF YOU ARE STUNG

Bees will always be an important part of our world. People need to know how to react to survive being swarmed. If you are stung, try to stay calm. If you are excited and your heart beats fast, it will make the venom spread more quickly throughout your body. Immediately remove any remaining stingers to prevent additional venom from being pumped into the bloodstream. Scrape off the stingers using your fingernail or a dull-edged knife or credit card—do not squeeze them.

When possible, keep stung areas below heart level. Apply cold compresses or covered ice cubes to the stings to decrease the pain. Take an antihistamine, like Benadryl.

Watch for serious symptoms, like trouble breathing, weakness, burning, itching, swelling, nausea, or rashes. If you start to have difficulty breathing, don't wait. Get medical attention as soon as possible. People who know they are allergic to bee venom often carry an EpiPen. This is a single shot of epinephrine, a medicine that can help stop fatal allergic reactions to bee venom.

If you see someone getting stung multiple times, call 911. Quick medical attention could mean the difference between life and death.

Right: People who know they are allergic to bee venom should always carry an EpiPen with them.

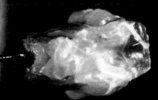

A bee's stinger in the tip of a thumb. For people who are allergic to bee venom, even one sting can cause the onset of anaphylactic shock.

GLOSSARY

ANAPHYLACTIC SHOCK

An over-reaction by a person's body to the introduction of venom, such as from a bee sting. The body sends large amounts of fluid to the stung area, causing swelling, pain, difficulty breathing, redness, and hives.

ANTIHISTAMINE

A medicine used to treat the symptoms of colds, hay fever, and other allergies, as well as the reactions people have to bee and wasp venom. It reduces swelling, congestion, and itchiness.

CARBON DIOXIDE

A colorless gas given off by humans and other mammals as they exhale. The chemical compound is made up of one carbon atom and two oxygen atoms. Its chemical symbol is CO_2.

ENTOMOLOGIST

A person who studies insects. Entomologists have been studying the development and spread of Africanized honeybees, also called "killer bees."

FERMENTED

Chemical changes that occur over time that result in the conversion of sugars to alcohol. Grapes go through a fermentation process to produce wine.

HYPODERMIC

A hollow needle used to inject fluid under the skin.

KILLER BEES

In 1956 in Brazil, South America, some colonies of European bees were crossed with African honeybees. The resulting strain of bees became known as Africanized honeybees, or AHBs. While the idea was to create a bee with increased honey production, the result was a bee that attacked humans faster and in greater numbers than European bees. The hybrid bees became known as "killer bees." AHBs entered the southern United States in 1990.

OLFACTORY RECEPTORS

Olfactory refers to a sense of smell. Receptors are the devices that receive the odor information. Olfactory receptors in bees are in their antennae.

PHEROMONE

A scented chemical substance given off by some insects that tells them how to behave. For example, an alarm pheromone tells bees to attack.

POLLINATION

An action where pollen is carried from one flower to another.

SUICIDE

To kill oneself.

SWARM

A large number of people or things. Swarm often refers to flying insects, such as bees. Bees will attack as a swarm in order to protect their hive.

VENOM

A poisonous liquid that some insects and reptiles, such as bees, snakes, and scorpions, use for killing prey and for defense.

INDEX

Bees are a vital part of our world. People need to know how to protect themselves from these important, yet sometimes dangerous, insects.